I Don't Like What's Happening

Liza Jane Bowling

BookLeaf Publishing

India | USA | UK

Made with ❤ on the BookLeaf Publishing Platform
www.bookleafpub.in
www.bookleafpub.com

for Linda

I'll be happy knowing this is but a taste

of what you've been waiting for

Acknowledgments

thank you

to my mom, for helping make this challenge
& collection possible for me and for being an
endless source of encouragement and love

to my sister, for always looking out for me,
pushing me in ways only a sister can push,
and for always being my big sister

to my dad, for loving me, guiding me, and
supporting me in every (and I mean EVERY)
area of my life, for never giving up or losing
hope even when I had

to my aunt Linda, for being one of the first
people to read my poetry and for being able
to understand me just a little bit more

to my dear friend Autumn, for always being a
source of support and inspiration for my

writing for all the years we've known each other

and finally to God, for creating me as I am, giving me this talent and passion for whatever His plans may be, nothing is impossible to Him, and none of this would be possible without Him.

Preface

To begin with, this is not how I imagined my first collection to get published. This isn't even my first collection. This book is a combination of poems that I wrote during graduate school and within the last month. This writing challenge from BookLeaf Publishing pushed my mind, emotions, and creativity to create something worth appreciating. While these poems may not be the most positive and uplifting (those will be for a future collection), they are still an extension of who I am and who I imagine myself to be.

My poetry dives into my past, present, and future, regardless of whether it happened, is happening, or will happen. My poetry exists to help make sense of my mind, but I love nothing more than when other people find safety and solace in my words, especially when they can't find them in their own. I always have a specific person, place, or experience in mind when I write each poem, but that's the beauty of poetry; the reader can have their interpretations.

The last few years have been a turbulent cycle of uncertainty, hope, and complacency. To say my life hasn't been turning out how I imagined is putting it lightly. No one can know what life will do, and these poems express those downward feelings in various ways.

Take my words however you will, however you need to. Break them apart, scatter them, let them grow in your mind. And remember that hope is coming with the rain.

Table of Contents

Homestead

Cherry pie and a glass of milk
on a Saturday morning

instead of swinging
in the hammock with you
My feet are firmly rooted
in the backyard.

Peering in the open window
and I see my shadow
running by.

Why didn't I run away
when the door was open?
Why did I keep baking
until the dough under my fingernails
hardened?

The vines around my wrists
pull me around,
showing me a home of blue skies
and open valleys.

A milk pie and cherry juice
seated neatly on a glass table,
far away from the hammock
and the open window.

Lament

I never wore my wedding dress.

Instead of being married to a man,
I'm being married to the ground.

Grayson, Kentucky, 1944

She left the light on for him,
hoping he'd find his way home.
She prayed for him
every night before she fell asleep,
asking God to keep him safe and warm.

Every morning she doubled the eggs,
poured an extra cup of coffee,
and placed the paper at the head of the table.

She twisted her necklace between her fingers,
humming a hymn while rocking on the porch.
Somewhere in the trees, a bird matched her tune.

Her eyes weighed as heavy as her heart.
She stopped rocking when the clouds rolled over.
The rain started,
and she knew he wasn't coming home.

Tonight

I don't want you to leave.
I don't want to be left here
all alone.
I don't want to be the only one
under our blanket.

I don't want to watch the snowfall
on my own.
You won't be here to tell me
it's time to go to bed.

I hope you'll be back in the morning.
I hope you'll wake up next to me.

I don't want to melt with the snow.

I Don't Like What's Happening

I had a dream growing up
that I would leave this place
and travel the world.

I would fall in love
with a handsome stranger,
settle down and raise kids.

I left for England when I was 23,
thinking that this was finally
when my life began.

I created a whole new life there.
I created a whole new person.
One who was comfortable
in her skin,
and one who was comfortable
letting someone else love her.

I had to go back home.
I had barely left and had already missed
the trains, the concerts, the nights out,
the man I had no trouble loving.

The only trace left of the person
I had become was with him,
and when he left,

that person left with him.

I was back to who I was
when I was dreaming.
I thought that's all
I would ever do.

I dreamt through rose-colored glasses
to create another person.
And as quickly as dreams happen,
mine started coming true again.

I thought this was it.
This was finally,
finally,
when my life began.

Korea would be different.
I wouldn't be coming home.
I'd fall in love all over again.
I'd settle into a new job,
a new life,
a new person.

Dreams only last for a few seconds.
They don't always happen
the way you dreamt them to.
They're filled with holes
that you don't know how to fill.

And dreams turn into nightmares.

I was there in the place
I had dreamt of for so long.
The cherry blossoms fluttered
and history flowed through the river
and flooded the streets.

I didn't want to leave.
But I would've died
if I had stayed.

I wouldn't be me anymore.

I would be a shell
of who I was.
All the lives I had lived,
all the places I had been,
dead and empty.

I knew I would miss the lake,
the trees, the concerts, the food,
the people, the simplicity of living.

And now as I get further away from my days
there,
I wonder if I made a mistake.

I want to go back,
I need to go back,
to try again,
to make sure it works this time.

The more I dream about being there,
the more I forget.

I forget that I lived there.
I forget that I started to build a life,
one that I wasn't ready to give up.

My dreams,
my memories,
the things I did,
that I tasted, touched, experienced,
are turning into shower thoughts.
They're separating in my hands
and dissolving into the water.

I can't remember if they were real.
And I hate knowing that they are.

Under the Harvest Moon

I dug a grave for someone
who was too afraid to dig her own.
I piled leaves on top of the dirt
until she was completely unseen to the world.
She wore a purple dress,
no shoes,
and a single locket around her neck.
She held daisies in her hands
and in her hair.
She stared up at me,
asking me to keep this a secret.
Her last words were said
with soft surrender
and I cried when there was nothing
left of her.

She said goodbye to no one,
and no one said goodbye to her.

Dancer

I wanted to dance around the room
with him.
I wanted to dim the lights,
close the curtains,
and throw the pillows and blankets
on the floor.

I wanted to unplug the clock,
to stop time and stay awake,
moving and loving without worry
of when to stop.

I wanted to sit next to him in the car.
I wanted to change to stations,
put the top down,
and let our hair tangle in the wind.

But I'm on the other side.
Neither here nor there,
with nothing pulling me in either direction.

I'm outside the window,
praying he doesn't close the curtains.
I'm sitting in the backseat,
unable to reach the radio,
unable to move his hair
out of his eyes.

All I can do is lay my head back,
close my eyes,
and finally go to sleep.

Tropic of Capricorn

You took hold of me little by little.
I never stood a chance.
I didn't want to let go.
Summers were always too cold.

Standing Still

It snowed in September.
The leaves on the ground
were buried underneath the weight.
Everything was quiet,
everything was peaceful.

And then

it stopped.
The snow melted.
The birds rested.
The sun filtered through the trees.

And then winter came.

Alexandria

My summers burned away
in the library that raised me.
The ceiling was charred among the smoke.
The pages curled
and the spines broke apart.
The doors locked into place,
burying me beneath the embers.

The library was still
and she was silent.

Alone Together

You were too tired on the way back home
to notice how much I was swerving.
I was too tired to notice
that you weren't listening.

We were both too busy
distracting our minds
to realize how dark
the road was.

I didn't even roll up the window
when the snow started to fall.

You turned the volume up
to drown me out.
I stopped talking
when the wind became too loud.

I could only see the lights
on the other side.
You couldn't even hear me crying.

Jericho

What do you do
when you've built your walls
up to the heavens
and someone
knocks
at the door?

You want to open up,
to let them see
everything you've kept
tucked away.

You want to let them in
because they'll understand
why you thought it best
to build your walls so high.

You're scared when they get closer
to finding their own way in,
until suddenly the sound of their voice
like trumpets
makes every wall crumble.

Stargazer

She looks at you like you made the stars.
And I guess,
in a way,
you did.

Before you,
she never looked up
at the night.
She didn't care about making wishes.

You came to her like a falling star.
Only then did she realize
that there were more beautiful things
in the sky
than on earth.

Eclipse

I am the moonshine
and you are the sunshine

but we can never
shine together

I Wanted to Leave

"We're either alone in the universe or
we're not," he told me once.

Even staring at the stars,
even grasping his hand,
I disagreed.

"No," I said.
"We're alone.
We've always been alone."

And I let go of his hand.

White Hot

My heart aches
every time you push your hair back.
My lungs cry out for your breath
every time you speak.
I feel a fever in my blood
every time you touch someone else.
There's a sharp pain in my bones
whenever you're not close to me.
I feel my eyes burn
every time I look at you.
I can feel my body slowly withering away
knowing you'll never be next to me.

Like the Sea

Instead of letting the freshwater
and the saltwater fight their way,
I jumped in
trying to get them to stop.

I stayed there,
underneath the surface,
looking up every now and then
to see the sun,
but realized it was just an illusion
from the water filling my lungs.

My eyes stayed open.
I saw the freshwater
and the saltwater.
Both sides were clear,
but I was stuck
in the murkiness of the middle.

Grain of Salt

I don't want you to tell me that you believe in me.
That's all you ever say.

Sometimes all I need is for you to agree with me.
Tell me to quit when I say I want to quit.
I'm tired of feeling like I have to get your
permission
to make my own decisions.

Constance

In May I drowned
in the lake behind your house.
The rain hit the surface
before I could close my eyes.

In September the stars moved
from behind the clouds
into the hands of your father.

In December the flowers bloomed
in your mother's garden.
The leaves grew bigger
every time it snowed.

When May came back,
the dock collapsed under your feet.

In the Corner of the Backyard

The ground is too cold to push up daisies.
Rocks have disturbed the dirt.
The only thing I can think of
is how you're no longer here.

Make Me Your Queen

His hands hung around my neck
like a string of pearls.
His voice covered my body
like a sheet.
I couldn't raise my voice,
only my hands.
My hair made a crown
around my head.
He spoke in words
that were meant to praise me.
I made him look me in the eyes,
worthy of being worshipped.

Prologue

I'm falling asleep
to the wind whistling
instead of you whispering.

She pushes the curtains aside
because you weren't here to close them.

The cars outside do nothing but scream,
but you're not here to laugh at your own joke.

The pigeon that lands on the windowsill
twists its head and looks at me,
asking me where you are.

He's not here, I tell the pigeon.
I roll over and am strangely content

when I feel the weight of it
lay down beside me and fall asleep.

Before Our Spring

The moon bled blue when it called you home.
The other stars dulled when I saw you next to
them.

Are you happy where you are?

That morning was bright and warm
and I was barely awake.
It was cold where you were,
but you felt safe.

You resembled the moon,
and now you've become her.

Don't worry, darling.
You did well down here.

L'affaire de Coeur

I always see you
out of the corner of my eye,
moving in the shadows,
a fleeting light.

I always hear you
when I turn my back,
right behind me,
moving around me.

You linger in the trees,
and I can only find you
through the fog of my breath.

I can only touch you
under the water,
when the steam touches the ceiling
and covers the mirror.

You're close enough
for me to smell your cologne,
to breathe in your scent.

You'll always be too far away
for me to be with you.

Mai

She went to Paris to find him.
Instead, she found heartache and rust
at the bottom of the Eiffel Tower.

She rubbed her fingers together
until there was nothing left but residue from an
itch.

All around her were neon signs

Il est là,
viens par ici.

She couldn't understand them.

She stumbled across the Pont d'Iéna
and dropped her heart into the water.

Je suis ici.
Regarde un peu plus près.

Paper Boutonnière

Take it with you
wherever you go,
and when people ask
what you're doing
say,
"I'm waiting for the rain."

Styx

Flowers bloomed overnight,
just like my feelings for you.
The rain fell
like tidal waves.

You were summer
and I was spring,
always one step behind you.

You were here
and then you weren't,
running away
every time I looked at you.

Thunder crashed
and you were electrified.
You lit up the night,
but only when the clouds
were covering me.

The flowers died overnight,
just like my feelings for you.

Midnight

Bitter was your touch
when I had already turned over
for the night.
I slipped through your hands
like honey.

It was dark and cold outside.
We met together
like the snow and the rain,
carelessly freezing in the wind.

My soul was ripped from my body.
You held it in your hands,
pulled it so thin,
it disappeared into the air.

I closed my eyes,
pulled the covers over my head,
and you drifted away.

Wonderland

You offered me a peach
with your fingers crossed behind your back.

So sweet it would be
to take a bite,
to let the juice drip down to the floor.

To descend into a dream,
fogged by the moonlight.

How maddening it would be
for you to take a bite
hovering over me.

You ripped the pearls off my neck,
made me choke on the pit.
I haven't stopped falling
through the fog.

Mir Wood

Her eyes glimmered
like a pale jewel in the moonlight.

Her long hair was braided
like vines wrapped around a tree.

Her hands were open,
inviting me to come closer.

Her dress swayed in the wind,
following her body.

Her feet danced above the ground,
cold and soft.

She didn't speak,
didn't smile.

She was gone
before the sun woke up.

Twin Flames

I was too young and too delirious
to realize we burned different colors.

You intoxicated the room
with a soft red halo
that floated above you.

People thought I was cold
with how blue I burned.

Your aura left nothing
to the imagination.
It was a burden for you
to try and figure out mine.

I buried our flames in a box.
The dirt melted into mud
and it sank deep beneath the earth.

I would've burned with you forever
if you hadn't already done the same.

Wild As She Grows

I don't know how long
I've been gone.

I left a note,
but no one's peeked in
or tapped on the glass.

Every day I watch
the ivy grow
from the ground to the roof.

And every day I tell myself
that I'll go back
when the vines get a little bit taller.

Anything Like Her

She leaves stars in her footprints
and fairy dust lingers
at her fingertips.

Her hair matches her lips
and her eyes match the sky.

She keeps you company,
lovely company,
and flowers bloom
in between your hands.

I could never pull your hands apart.
I could never leave traces
of myself for you to linger on.
I could never be anything like her.

Monsoon

It rained
and you were the water
and I was
drowning
in you.

Say Yes

Do you want the moon?
I'll pull down the moon for you.
I'll drag her to the edge of the shores,
drown the land in her waters.
You just have to say yes.

Or do you want the sun?
I'll burn her up into billions of marbles,
all filled with her flames and the stars
that surrounded her.
She'll radiate forever in your hands.

I'll give you the stars.
I'll pick them out of the sky
and sprinkle them over everything you touch.

You just have to say yes.